THE
OXFORD
CHRISTMAS
CAROL
BOOK

THE OXFORD CHRISTMAS CAROL BOOK

Music Department
OXFORD UNIVERSITY PRESS
Oxford and New York

Oxford University Press, Walton Street, Oxford OX2 6DP, England
Oxford University Press, 200 Madison Avenue, New York, NY 10016, USA
Oxford New York Toronto
Delhi Bombay Calcutta Madras Karachi
Petaling Jaya Singapore Hong Kong Tokyo
Nairobi Dar es Salaam Cape Town
Melbourne Auckland
and associated companies in
Berlin Ibadan

British Library Cataloguing in Publication Data
The Oxford Christmas carol book.
1. Christmas carols in English—Collections
783.6'552
ISBN 0–19–313132–3

Oxford is a trade mark of Oxford University Press

Printed in Hong Kong

CONTENTS

THE
OXFORD
CHRISTMAS
CAROL
BOOK

Gloria, gloria

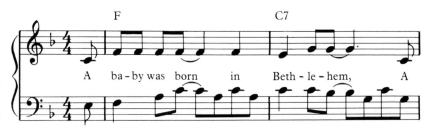

A ba-by was born in Beth-le-hem, A

ba-by was born in Beth-le-hem, A ba-by was born in

Beth-le-hem, It was Je-sus Christ, our Lord.

Glo-ri-a, Glo-ri-a in ex-cel-sis

De - o. Glo - ri - a,

Glo - ri - a, sing glo - ry to God on high.

IVOR GOLBY

2 They laid him in a manger (*repeat three times*)
   Where the oxen fed on hay.

   Gloria, Gloria in excelsis Deo.
   Gloria, Gloria, sing glory to God on high.

3 Some shepherds heard the glad tidings (*repeat*)
   From an angel in the sky.

4 They left their flocks a-sleeping (*repeat*)
   And hurried to Bethlehem.

5 Three wise men came from far lands, (*repeat*)
   They were guided by a star.

6 They laid their gifts before him (*repeat*)
   And worshipped on bended knee.

7 Then everybody be happy (*repeat*)
   On the birthday of our Lord.

IVOR GOLBY

 # way in a manger

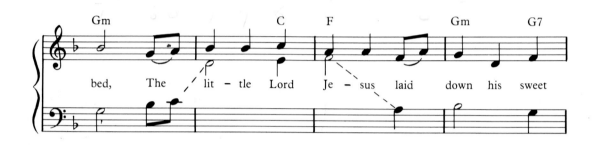

A — way in a man -ger, no crib for a

bed, The lit – tle Lord Je – sus laid down his sweet

head. The stars in the bright sky looked down where he

lay, The lit – tle Lord Je – sus a – sleep on the hay.

W. J. KIRKPATRICK

2 The cattle are lowing, the baby awakes,
But little Lord Jesus no crying he makes.
I love thee, Lord Jesus! Look down from the sky,
And stay by my side until morning is nigh.

3 Be near me, Lord Jesus; I ask thee to stay
Close by me for ever, and love me, I pray.
Bless all the dear children in thy tender care,
And fit us for heaven, to live with thee there.

child this day is born

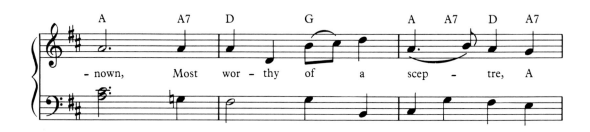

A child this day is born, A child of high re-

-nown, Most wor-thy of a scep - tre, A

scep - tre and a crown. No - well, No - well, No -

- well, No - well sing all we may, Be -

6

| D | G | | A | A7 | D | A7 | D | G | D | A | | D |

- cause the King of all kings Was born this bless - ed day.

TRADITIONAL ENGLISH CAROL

2 These tidings shepherds hear,
In field watching their fold,
Were by an angel unto them
That night revealed and told:

Nowell, Nowell, Nowell,
Nowell, sing all we may,
Because the King of all kings
Was born this blessed day.

3 To whom the angel spoke,
Saying, 'Be not afraid;
Be glad, poor silly shepherds
Why are you so dismayed?'

4 'For lo! I bring you tidings
Of gladness and of mirth,
Which cometh to all people by
This holy infant's birth':

5 Then was there with the angel
An host incontinent
Of heavenly bright soldiers
Which from the Highest was sent:

6 Lauding the Lord our God,
And his celestial King;
All glory be in paradise,
This heavenly host did sing:

7 And as the angel told them,
So to them did appear;
They found the young child, Jesus
Christ,
With Mary, his mother dear:

The words and tune are found in Sandys' 'Christmas
Carols' (see note on p. 27) where twenty-one verses are
included! The word 'silly' in verse 3 meant 'simple'.

Angels, from the realms of glory

An-gels, from the realms of glo - ry, Wing your flight o'er

all the earth; Ye who sang cre - a - tion's sto - ry

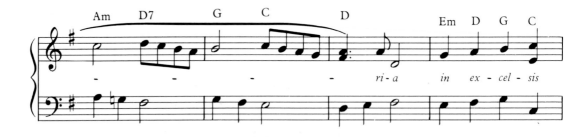

Now pro - claim Mes - si - ah's birth: *Glo* - -

- - - - *ri - a in ex - cel - sis*

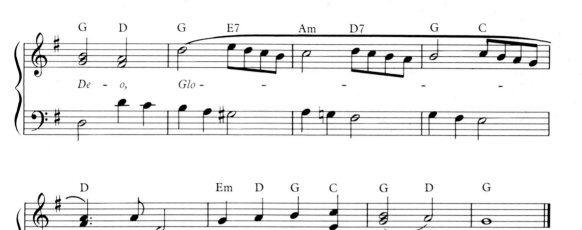

De - o, Glo- - - - - -

- ri - a in ex - cel - sis De - o.

TRADITIONAL FRENCH TUNE

2 Shepherds, in the field abiding,
Watching o'er your flocks by night,
God with man is now residing;
Yonder shines the infant light:

Gloria in excelsis Deo,
Gloria in excelsis Deo.

3 Sages, leave your contemplations;
Brighter visions beam afar;
See the great Desire of Nations;
Ye have seen his natal star:

4 Saints before the altar bending,
Watching long in hope and fear,
Suddenly the Lord, descending,
In his temple shall appear:

5 Though an infant now we view him,
He shall fill his Father's throne,
Gather all the nations to him;
Every knee shall then bow down:

JAMES MONTGOMERY

The words of Montgomery's nineteenth-century hymn are combined
with the music of the old French carol, 'Les anges dans nos
campagnes'. The refrain, 'Gloria in excelsis Deo', is taken from
the French carol; Montgomery's refrain is 'Come and worship
Christ the new-born King'.

As with gladness

As with glad-ness men of old Did the guid-ing star be-hold, As with joy they hailed its light, Lead-ing on-ward, beam-ing bright, So, most gra-cious God, may we Ev-er-more be led to thee.

C. KOCHER

2 As with joyful steps they sped,
   To that lowly manger-bed,
   There to bend the knee before
   Him whom heaven and earth adore,
   So may we with willing feet
   Ever seek thy mercy-seat.

3 As they offered gifts most rare
   At that manger rude and bare,
   So may we with holy joy,
   Pure, and free from sin's alloy,
   All our costliest treasures bring,
   Christ, to thee our heavenly King.

4 Holy Jesu, every day
   Keep us in the narrow way;
   And, when earthly things are past,
   Bring our ransomed souls at last
   Where they need no star to guide,
   Where no clouds thy glory hide.

W. C. DIX

A virgin most pure

A vir - gin most pure as the pro - phets do tell,

Hath brought forth a ba - by, as it hath be - fell; To

be our Re - deem - er from death, hell, and sin, Which A - dam's trans-

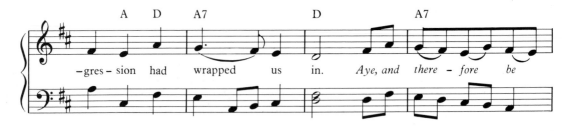

-gres - sion had wrapped us in. Aye, and there - fore be

mer - ry; Re - joice, and be you mer - ry; Set sor - row a-

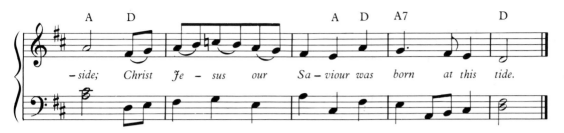

-side; Christ Je - sus our Sa - viour was born at this tide.

ENGLISH TRADITIONAL CAROL

2   The Kings of all kings to this world being brought,
Small store of fine linen to wrap him was sought;
And when she had swaddled her young son so sweet,
Within an ox-manger she laid him to sleep.

Aye, and therefore be merry;
Rejoice, and be you merry;
Set sorrow aside;
Christ Jesus our Saviour was born at this tide.

3   Then God sent an angel from heaven so high,
To certain poor shepherds in fields where they lie,
And bade them no longer in sorrow to stay,
Because that our Saviour was born on this day.

4   Then presently after the shepherds did spy
A number of angels that stood in the sky;
They joyfully talked and sweetly did sing,
'To God be all glory our heavenly King.'

This is one of the many traditional carols which survived thanks to
having been published in 1822 by Davies Gilbert in 'Some
Ancient Christmas Carols with tunes to which they were formally
sung in the West of England'. Gilbert's many activities included
being a London lawyer, Member of Parliament for Bodmin, and
President of the Royal Society.

Come, leave your sheep

Come leave your sheep, Your ewes with lambs a-feed-ing, O shep-herds, hear Our mes-sage of good cheer; No long-er weep; The an-gel-ti-dings heed-ing, To Beth-lem haste a-way! Our Lord, our Lord, Our Lord is born this hap-py

14

day. Our Lord, our Lord, Our Lord is born this hap - py day.

TRADITIONAL FRENCH CAROL

2 He lieth there
   Within a lowly manger;
   An infant poor
   He languisheth full sore.
   God's loving care
   Hath saved us all from danger
   And brought us to his fold:
   Now own, now own
   His faithful love revealed of old.

3 Ye sages three
   Arrayed in royal splendour,
   Your homage pay;
   A king is born this day.
   The star ye see
   Its radiance must surrender
   Before our Sun most bright;
   Your gifts, your gifts,
   Your gifts are precious in his sight.

4 Come Holy Ghost,
   Of blessings source eternal,
   Our souls inspire
   With thy celestial fire;
   The heavenly host
   Praise Christ the Lord supernal
   And sing the peace on earth
   God gives, God gives,
   God gives us by his holy birth.

TR. JOHN RUTTER

*Many French noëls or carols have become popular in English
translations. This example is a version of the old French carol,
'Quittez, pasteurs'.*

Deck the hall

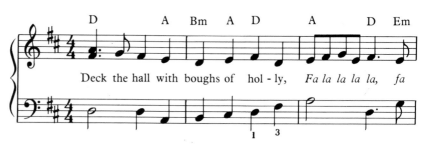

Deck the hall with boughs of hol - ly, *Fa la la la la, fa*

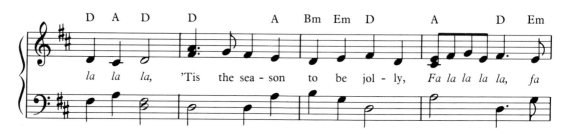

la la la, 'Tis the sea - son to be jol - ly, *Fa la la la la, fa*

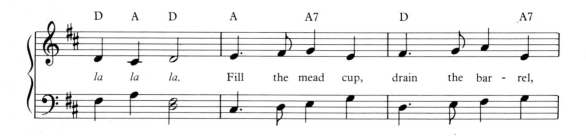

la la la. Fill the mead cup, drain the bar - rel,

Fa la la la, fa la la la, Troll the an - cient

Christ - mas ca - rol, *Fa la la la la, fa la la la.*

TRADITIONAL WELSH CAROL

2   See the flowing bowl before us,
    Fa la la la la, fa la la la,
    Strike the harp and join the chorus,
    Fa la la la la, fa la la la.
    Follow me in merry measure,
    Fa la la la la, fa la la la,
    While I sing of beauty's treasure,
    Fa la la la la, fa la la la.

3   Fast away the old year passes,
    Fa la la la la, fa la la la,
    Hail the new, ye lads and lasses,
    Fa la la la la, fa la la la.
    Laughing, quaffing all together,
    Fa la la la la, fa la la la,
    Heedless of the wind and weather,
    Fa la la la la, fa la la la.

*A traditional English version of the Welsh
New Year's Eve carol, 'Nos Galan'.*

Ding Dong! merrily on high

Ding dong! mer-ri-ly on high In heav'n the bells are

ring - ing: Ding dong! ve-ri-ly the sky Is riv'n with an-gels

sing - ing. Glo - - - - - - -

- - - ri - a, Ho - san - na in ex - cel - sis!

16TH-CENTURY FRENCH TUNE

2 E'en so here below, below,
   Let steeple bells be swungen,
   And i-o, i-o, i-o,
   By priest and people sungen:
   Gloria, Hosanna in excelsis!

3 Pray you, dutifully prime
   Your matin chime, ye ringers;
   May you beautifully rime
   Your eve-time song, ye singers.
   Gloria, Hosanna in excelsis!

G. R. WOODWARD

The tune is from Arbeau's dancing tutor 'Orchésographie' (1588). Some of these dances are well known today from their use in Peter Warlock's Capriol Suite.

18

ingle, bells

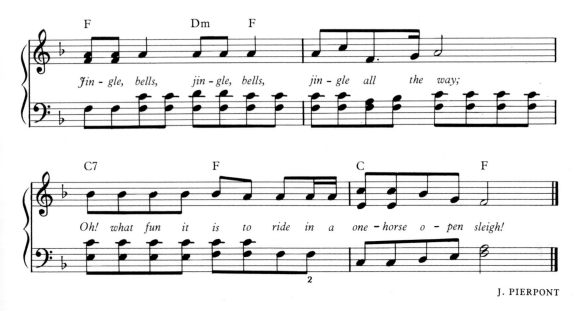

Jin - gle, bells, jin - gle, bells, jin - gle all the way;

Oh! what fun it is to ride in a one - horse o - pen sleigh!

J. PIERPONT

2   Now the ground is white;
Go it while you're young,
Take the girls tonight,
And sing this sleighing song.
Just get a bob-tailed bay,
Two-forty for his speed;
Then hitch him to an open sleigh
And crack! you'll take the lead.

Jingle, bells, jingle, bells, jingle all the way;
Oh, what fun it is to ride in a one-horse open sleigh!
Jingle, bells, jingle, bells, jingle all the way;
Oh, what fun it is to ride in a one-horse open sleigh!

Down in yon forest

Down in yon fo-rest there stands a hall: *The*

bells of pa-ra-dise I heard them ring: It's cov-er'd all o-ver with

pur-ple and pall: *And I love my Lord Je-sus a-bove a-ny-thing.*

TRADITIONAL ENGLISH CAROL

2   In that hall there stands a bed:
    The bells of paradise I heard them ring:
    It's covered all over with scarlet so red:
    And I love my Lord Jesus above anything.

3   At the bed-side there lies a stone:
    Which the sweet Virgin Mary knelt upon:

4   Under that bed there runs a flood:
    The one half runs water, the other runs blood:

5   At the bed's foot there grows a thorn:
    Which ever blows blossom since he was born:

6   Over that bed the moon shines bright:
    Denoting our Saviour was born this night:

The words and tune were collected by R. Vaughan Williams from a singer in Derbyshire. As well as the passion of Christ and the eucharist, there are references to the legend of the Holy Grail and the Glastonbury thorn.

he yodler's carol

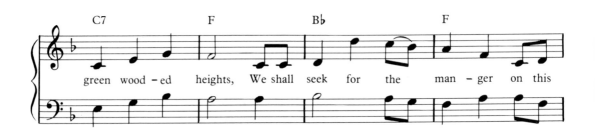

From the snow crowned moun-tain mea-dows, from the

green wood-ed heights, We shall seek for the man-ger on this

calm, ho-ly night. Let's sing 'Hol-di-ri-o' for a ca-rol sweet and clear,

'Hol-di-ri-o' as on we go; Then comes 'Hol-di-ri-o' for an

e – cho soft and clear, far a – cross the snow.

TRADITIONAL

2 Little stars shall be our candles,
   as we journey this night—
   Tiny diamonds in the heavens—
   we'll not want for a light.
   We sing 'Holdirio' for a carol sweet and clear,
   'Holdirio' as on we go;
   Then comes 'Holdirio' for an echo soft and clear,
   far across the snow.

3 We have found him, little Jesus,
   and we kneel by his bed.
   See the bright star o'er his cradle;
   radiant light crowns his head!
   We'll sing 'Holdirio' for a little lullaby,
   'Holdirio' so soft and low.
   Now on tiptoe go, do not make a single sound;
   then home across the snow.

MARY E. CALDWELL

od rest you merry, gentlemen

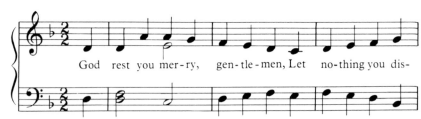

God rest you mer-ry, gen-tle-men, Let no-thing you dis-

-may, For Je - sus Christ our Sa - viour was born up - on this

day, To save us all from Sa - tan's power When we were gone a-

-stray: O ti - dings of com - fort and joy, *Com-fort and*

joy, O ti - dings of com - fort and joy.

TRADITIONAL ENGLISH CAROL

26

2 In Bethlehem in Jewry
This blessed babe was born,
And laid within a manger,
Upon this blessed morn;
The which his mother Mary
Nothing did take in scorn:

O tidings of comfort and joy,
Comfort and joy,
O tidings of comfort and joy.

3 From God our heavenly Father
A blessed angel came,
And unto certain shepherds
Brought tidings of the same,
How that in Bethlehem was born
The Son of God by name:

4 'Fear not,' then said the Angel,
'Let nothing you affright,
This day is born a Saviour,
Of virtue, power, and might;
So frequently to vanquish all
The friends of Satan quite':

5 The shepherds at those tidings
Rejoiced much in mind,
And left their flocks a-feeding,
In tempest, storm, and wind,
And went to Bethlehem straightway
This blessed babe to find:

6 And when they came to Bethlehem,
Where our sweet Savoiur lay,
They found him in a manger,
Where oxen feed on hay;
His mother Mary kneeling,
Unto the Lord did pray:

7 Now to the Lord sing praises
All you within this place,
And with true love and brotherhood
Each other now embrace;
This holy tide of Christmas
All others doth deface:

As well as Davies Gilbert (see note on p. 13), William Sandys was
active collecting traditional carols in the south-west of England.
He published his collection, 'Christmas Carols Ancient and
Modern' in 1833, and included the words of this carol.
The tune comes from London. In the first line, the comma between
'merry' and 'gentlemen' is correct: 'God rest you merry' means
'God keep you merry'.

 **o tell it on the mountain**

Go tell it on the mount-ain, Ov-er the hills and

ev-'ry-where, Go tell it on the mount-ain that Je-sus Christ is

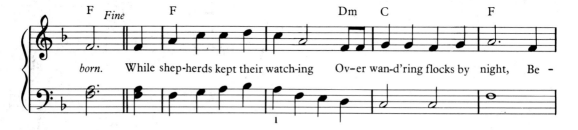

born. While shep-herds kept their watch-ing Ov-er wan-d'ring flocks by night, Be-

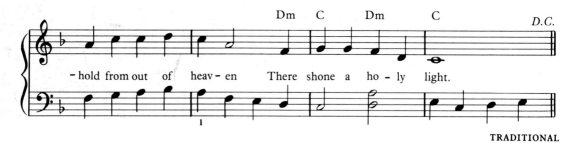

-hold from out of heav-en There shone a ho-ly light.

TRADITIONAL

Go, tell it on the mountain,
Over the hills and everywhere,
Go, tell it on the mountain
That Jesus Christ is born.

2 And lo, when they had seen it,
They all bowed down and prayed,
They travelled on together
To where the babe was laid.

Good King Wenceslas

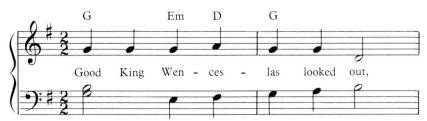

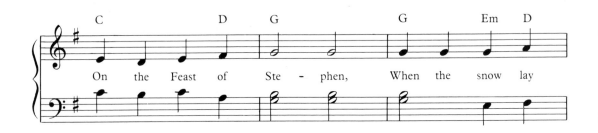

Good King Wen - ces - las looked out,

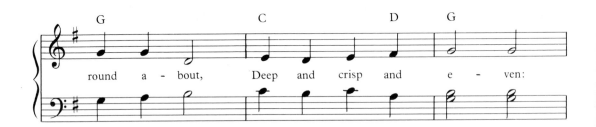

On the Feast of Ste - phen, When the snow lay

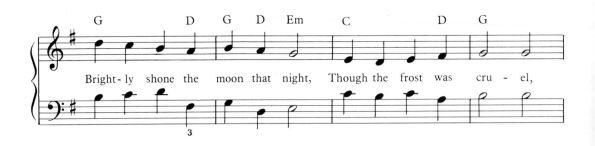

round a - bout, Deep and crisp and e - ven:

Bright - ly shone the moon that night, Though the frost was cru - el,

When a poor man came in sight, Gath-'ring win-ter fu - el.

TUNE FROM PIAE CANTIONES

2 'Hither, page, and stand by me,
   If thou know'st it, telling,
   Yonder peasant, who is he?
   Where and what his dwelling?'
   'Sire, he lives a good league hence,
   Underneath the mountain,
   Right against the forest fence,
   By St. Agnes' fountain.'

3 'Bring me flesh, and bring me wine,
   Bring me pine-logs hither:
   Thou and I will see him dine,
   When we bear them thither.'
   Page and monarch, forth they went,
   Forth they went together;
   Through the rude wind's wild lament
   And the bitter weather.

4 'Sire, the night is darker now,
   And the wind blows stronger;
   Fails my heart, I know not how;
   I can go no longer.'
   'Mark my footsteps, good my page;
   Tread thou in them boldly:
   Thou shalt find the winter's rage
   Freeze thy blood less coldly.'

5 In his master's steps he trod,
   Where the snow lay dinted;
   Heat was in the very sod
   Which the Saint had printed.
   Therefore, Christian men, be sure,
   Wealth or rank possessing,
   Ye who now will bless the poor,
   Shall yourselves find blessing.

J. M. NEALE

The tune is a thirteenth-century spring-time carol, 'Tempus adest
floridum'. This carol is one of the 74 songs found in the Finnish
collection, 'Piae cantiones', published by Theodoricus Petri
Nylandensis in 1582. In the mid-nineteenth century a copy of the
book was given to John Mason Neale, who provided English
words to many of the carols.

Wexford carol

Good peo-ple all this Christ-mas-time, Con-si-der well and bear in mind What our good God for us has done, In send-ing his be-lo-ved Son. With Ma-ry ho-ly we should pray To God with love this Christ-mas Day; In Beth-le-hem up-on that morn There

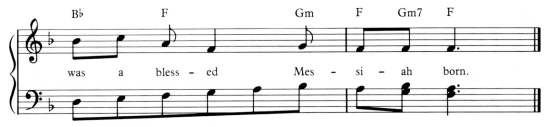

was   a   bless—ed   Mes—si—ah   born.

TRADITIONAL IRISH CAROL

2   Near Bethlehem did shepherds keep
    Their flocks of lambs and feeding sheep;
    To whom God's angels did appear,
    Which put the shepherds in great fear.
    'Prepare and go', the angels said,
    'To Bethlehem, be not afraid;
    For there you'll find, this happy morn,
    A princely babe, sweet Jesus born.'

3   With thankful heart and joyful mind,
    The shepherds went the babe to find,
    And as God's angel had foretold,
    They did our Saviour Christ behold.
    Within a manger he was laid,
    And by his side the virgin maid,
    Attending on the Lord of life,
    Who came on earth to end all strife.

This carol was collected from a folksinger in County Wexford.
The music is thought to be from Ireland, although some of the
words are also found in traditional English sources.

He is born

G   Em

He is born the di-vine Christ-child, Sound forth the o-boes with

D   Em   D   G

pipes re - ply - ing; He is born the di - vine Christ - child,

Em   D   G   *Fine*   G

Sing we praise to the in - fant mild. More than four thou - sand

Am   D   G   Am   G   D

years on earth, Seers his ad - vent were pro - phe - sy - ing;

G   Am   D   G   Am   G   D   *D.C.*

More than four thou-sand years on earth, Man a - wait - ed this joy - ous birth.

1

TRADITIONAL FRENCH CAROL

34

He is born the divine Christ-child,
Sound forth the oboes with pipes replying;
He is born the divine Christ-child,
Sing we praise to the infant mild.

2 O what beauty and charm are thine,
  Heavenly grace to our hearts supplying;
  O what beauty and charm are thine,
  O what sweetness thou Child divine!

3 In a manger thou deignst to be,
  Straw the bed where on thou art lying;
  In a manger thou deignst to be,
  Man awaited this joyous birth.

4 Jesu, King, whom we bow before,
  Yet an infant all power denying;
  Jesu, King, whom we bow before,
  Rule our hearts now and evermore.

TR. DAVID WILLCOCKS

A translation of the traditional French carol, 'Il est né le divin enfant'.

# ark! the herald-angels sing

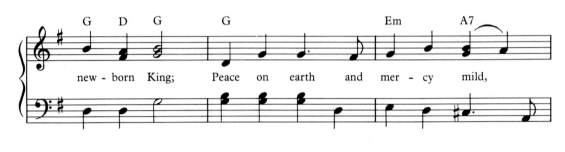

Hark! the he - rald - an - gels sing Glo - ry to the

new - born King; Peace on earth and mer - cy mild,

God and sin - ners re - con - ciled: Joy - ful all ye na - tions rise,

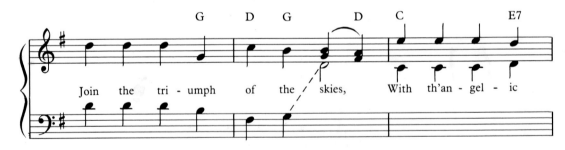

Join the tri - umph of the skies, With th'an - gel - ic

Am E Am   D D7 G   G D G   C   G

host pro-claim, Christ is born in Beth - le - hem. *Hark! the he - rald -*

Am E Am   D D7 G   G D G

- an - gels sing Glo - ry to the new - born King.

MENDELSSOHN

2 Christ, by highest heaven adored,
Christ, the everlasting Lord,
Late in time behold him come
Offspring of a virgin's womb:
Veiled in flesh the Godhead see,
Hail the incarnate Deity!
Pleased as Man with man to dwell,
Jesus, our Emmanuel.

Hark! the herald-angels sing
Glory to the new-born King.

3 Hail the heaven-born Prince of peace!
Hail the Sun of Righteousness!
Light and life to all he brings,
Risen with healing in his wings;
Mild he lays his glory by,
Born that man no more may die,
Born to raise the sons of earth,
Born to give them second birth.

CHARLES WESLEY AND OTHERS

The music was adapted by W. H. Cummings from a chorus in
Mendelssohn's 'Festgesang'.

assail song

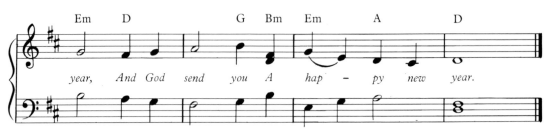

TRADITIONAL ENGLISH CAROL

38

2 We are not daily beggars
That beg from door to door,
But we are neighbours' children
Whom you have seen before:

Love and joy come to you,
And to you your wassail too,
And God bless you, and send you
A happy new year.

3 God bless the master of this house,
Likewise the mistress too;
And all the little children
That round the table go:

4 Good Master and good Mistress,
While you're sitting by the fire,
Pray think of us poor children
Who are wandering in the mire:

The music is from Yorkshire. For the meaning of the word
'wassail', see note on p. 109.

How far is it to Bethlehem?

How far is it to Beth - le -hem? Not ve - ry

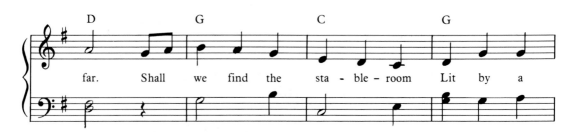

far. Shall we find the sta - ble - room Lit by a

Verse 4 starts here

star? Can we see the lit - tle child, Is he with -

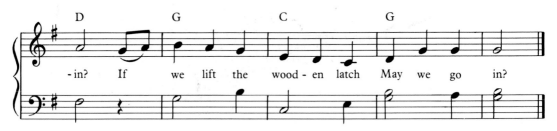

-in? If we lift the wood - en latch May we go in?

TRADITIONAL ENGLISH MELODY

2 May we stroke the creatures there,
 Ox, ass or sheep?
 May we peep like them and see
 Jesus asleep?
 If we touch his tiny hand
 Will he awake?
 Will he know we've come so far
 Just for his sake?

3 Great kings have precious gifts,
   And we have naught,
   Little smiles and little tears
   Are all we brought.
   For all weary children
   Mary must weep.
   Here, on his bed of straw
   Sleep, children, sleep.

4 God in his mother's arms,
   Babes in the byre,
   Sleep, as they sleep who find
   Their heart's desire.

FRANCES CHESTERTON

An English folk-tune, 'Stowey', with modern words.

 saw three ships

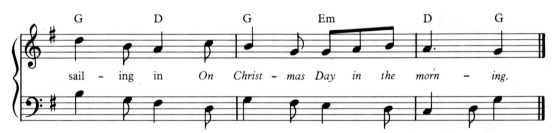

TRADITIONAL ENGLISH CAROL

2　And what was in those ships all three?
　On Christmas Day, on Christmas Day,
　And what was in those ships all three?
　On Christmas Day in the morning.

3　Our Saviour Christ and his lady.

4　Pray, whither sailed those ships all three?

5　O, they sailed into Bethlehem.

6　And all the bells on earth shall ring.

7　And all the angels in heaven shall sing.

8　And all the souls on earth shall sing.

9　Then let us all rejoice amain!

*This, one of the most popular of traditional carols, is found with
variants from many different parts of England, including Sandys'
collection (see note on p. 27).*

 *n dulci jubilo*

In dul - ci ju - bi - lo Let

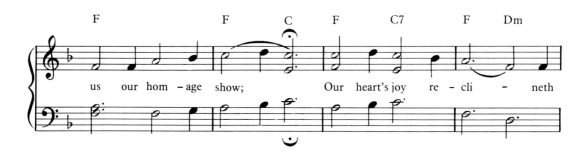

us our hom – age show; Our heart's joy re - cli – neth

In prae - se – pi – o And like a bright star

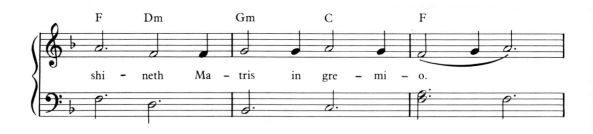

shi – neth Ma – tris in gre – mi – o.

OLD GERMAN CAROL

2 O Jesu parvule!
   My heart is sore for thee!
   Hear me, I beseech thee,
   O Puer optime!
   My prayer let it reach thee,
   O Princeps gloriae!
   Trahe me post te!
   Trahe me post te!

3 O Patris caritas,
   O Nati lenitas!
   Deeply were we stainèd
   Per nostra crimina;
   But thou for us hast gainèd
   Coelorum gaudia.
   O that we were there!
   O that we were there!

4 Ubi sunt gaudia,
   If that they be not there?
   There are angels singing
   Nova cantica,
   There the bells are ringing
   In Regis curia:
   O that we were there!
   O that we were there!

TR. R. L. PEARSALL

*This is an example of a macaronic text, i.e. in more than one
language. The fourteenth-century German tune has been
arranged by many composers, including J. S. Bach, and it is
also found in 'Piae Cantiones' (see note on p. 31), but is perhaps
best known through its choral arrangement by Pearsall.
A fourteenth-century manuscript states that the words were sung by
angels to the mystic, Henry Suso.*

 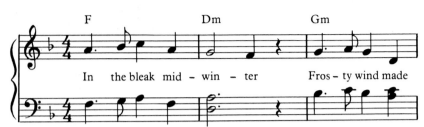

In the bleak mid-winter

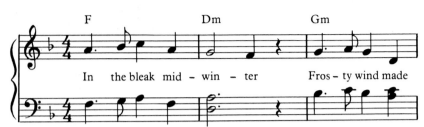

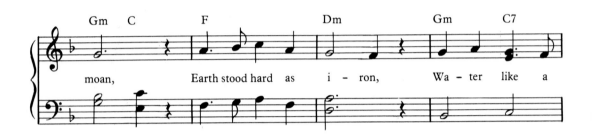

| F | | Dm | | Gm |
In the bleak mid – win – ter Fros – ty wind made

| Gm | C | F | | Dm | | Gm | C7 |
moan, Earth stood hard as i – ron, Wa – ter like a

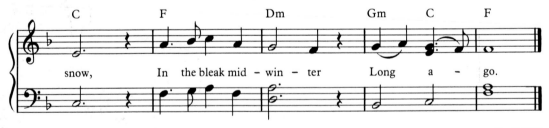

| F | | Bb | F | Bb | Dm | F | Gm |
stone; Snow had fal – len, snow on snow, Snow on

| C | F | | Dm | | Gm | C | F |
snow, In the bleak mid – win – ter Long a – go.

G. HOLST

2 Our God, heaven cannot hold him
Nor earth sustain;
Heaven and earth shall flee away
When he comes to reign:
In the bleak mid-winter
A stable-place sufficed
The Lord God Almighty
Jesus Christ.

3 Enough for him, whom cherubim
Worship night and day,
A breastful of milk,
And a mangerful of hay;
Enough for him, whom angels
Fall down before,
The ox and ass and camel
Which adore.

4 What can I give him
Poor as I am?
If I were a shepherd
I would bring a lamb;
If I were a wise man
I would do my part;
Yet what I can I give him—
Give my heart.

CHRISTINA ROSSETTI

*The music, 'Cranham', is one of three
hymns which Gustav Holst wrote
especially for 'The English Hymnal', at
the request of R. Vaughan Williams.*

Infant holy

Infant holy, Infant lowly, For his bed a cattle stall; Oxen lowing, Little knowing Christ the Babe is Lord of all. Swift are winging Angels singing, Nowells ringing, Tidings bringing,

Christ the Babe is Lord of all, Christ the Babe is Lord of all.

POLISH TUNE

2 Flocks were sleeping, shepherds keeping
  Vigil till the morning new;
  Saw the glory, heard the story,
  Tidings of a gospel true.
  Thus rejoicing, free from sorrow,
  Praises voicing, greet the morrow,
  Christ the Babe was born for you!
  Christ the Babe was born for you!

TR. EDITH M. REED

It came upon the midnight clear

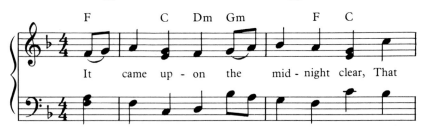

It came up - on the mid - night clear, That

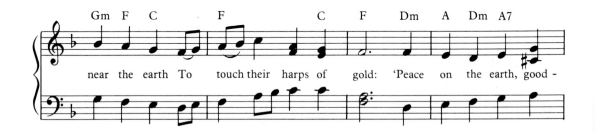

glo - rious song of old, From an - gels bend - ing

near the earth To touch their harps of gold: 'Peace on the earth, good -

- will to men, From heav'n's all - gra - cious King!' The

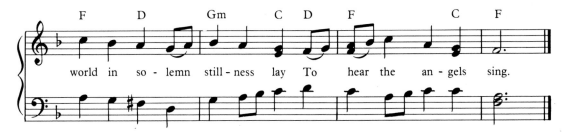

world in so - lemn still - ness lay To hear the an - gels sing.

TRADITIONAL ENGLISH TUNE
ADAPTED BY ARTHUR SULLIVAN

2 Still through the cloven skies they come,
   With peaceful wings unfurled;
   And still their heavenly music floats
   O'er all the weary world;
   Above its sad and lowly plains
   They bend on hovering wing;
   And ever o'er its Babel sounds
   The blessed angels sing.

3 Yet with the woes of sin and strife
   The world has suffered long;
   Beneath the angel-strain have rolled
   Two thousand years of wrong;
   And man, at war with man, hears not
   The love-song which they bring:
   O hush the noise ye men of strife,
   And hear the angels sing!

4 And ye, beneath life's crushing load,
   Whose forms are bending low,
   Who toil along the climbing way
   With painful steps and slow,
   Look now! for glad and golden hours
   Come swiftly on the wing;
   O rest beside the weary road,
   And hear the angels sing!

5 For lo! the days are hastening on,
   By prophet-bards foretold,
   When, with the ever-circling years,
   Comes round the age of gold;
   When peace shall over all the earth
   Its ancient splendours fling,
   And the whole world give back the song
   Which now the angels sing.

E. H. SEARS

Sullivan took the old Herefordshire carol tune, 'Eardisley',
and arranged and extended it.

oy to the world!

Joy to the world, the Lord is come!

Let earth re-ceive her King; Let eve-ry heart pre-

-pare him room, And heav'n and na-ture sing, And

heav'n and na-ture sing, And heav'n, and heav'n and na-ture sing.

LOWELL MASON

52

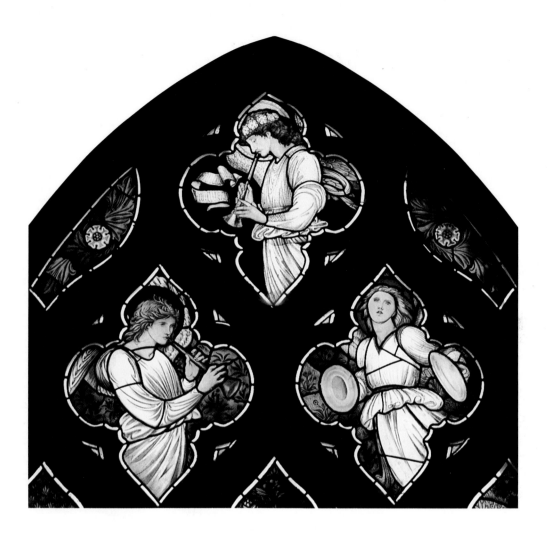

2   Joy to the world! the Saviour reigns;
     Let men their songs employ,
     While fields and floods, rocks, hills and plains
     Repeat the sounding joy, repeat the sounding joy,
     Repeat, repeat the sounding joy.

3   He rules the world with truth and grace,
     And makes the nations prove
     The glories of his righteousness
     And wonders of his love, and wonders of his love,
     And wonders, wonders of his love.

ISAAC WATTS

Lowell Mason based this music on that of Handel; Isaac Watts'
words are based on Psalm 98.

King Jesus hath a garden

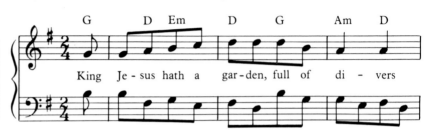

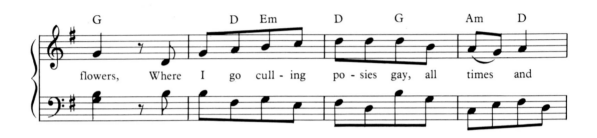

King Je-sus hath a gar-den, full of di — vers

flowers, Where I go cull-ing po-sies gay, all times and

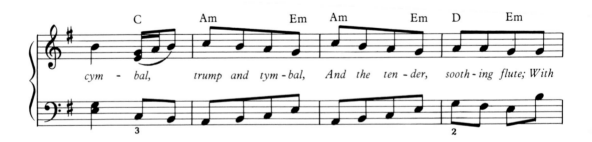

hours. *There naught is heard but Pa-ra-dise bird, Harp, dul-ci-mer, lute, With*

cym — bal,   trump and tym-bal,   And the ten-der,   sooth-ing flute; With

TRADITIONAL DUTCH TUNE

2 The Lily, white in blossom there, is Chastity:
The Violet, with sweet perfume, Humility.

There naught is heard but Paradise bird,
Harp, dulcimer, lute,
With cymbal, trump and tymbal,
And the tender, soothing flute;
With cymbal, trump and tymbal,
And the tender, soothing flute.

3 The bonny Damask-rose is known as Patïence:
The blithe and thrifty Marygold, Obedïence.

4 The Crown Imperial bloometh too in yonder place,
'Tis Charity, of stock divine, the flower of grace.

5 Yet, 'mid the brave, the bravest prize of all may claim
The Star of Bethlem—Jesus—blessed be his Name!

6 Ah! Jesu Lord, my heal and weal, my bliss complete,
Make thou my heart thy garden-plot, fair, trim and neat.

That I may hear this musick clear:
Harp, dulcimer, lute,
With cymbal, trump and tymbal,
And the tender, soothing flute;
With cymbal, trump and tymbal,
And the tender, soothing flute.

TR. G. R. WOODWARD

'Heer Jesus heeft een hofken' is a seventeenth-century Dutch carol.

ittle Jesus, sweetly sleep

Lit – tle Je – sus, sweet-ly sleep, do not stir;

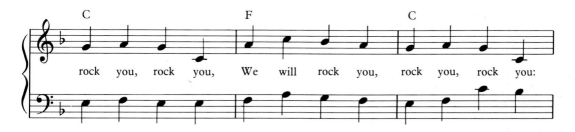

We will lend a coat of fur, We will rock you,

rock you, rock you, We will rock you, rock you, rock you:

See the fur to keep you warm, Snug-ly round your ti – ny form.

TRADITIONAL CZECH CAROL

2 Mary's little baby, sleep, sweetly sleep,
   Sleep in comfort, slumber deep;
   We will rock you, rock you, rock you,
   We will rock you, rock you, rock you:
   We will serve you all we can,
   Darling, darling little man.

TR. PERCY DEARMER

Coventry carol

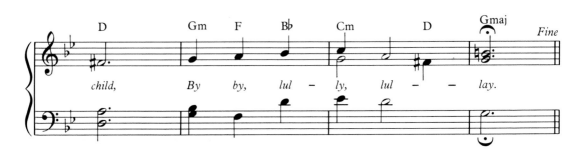

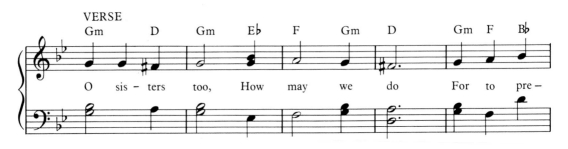

whom we do sing, By by, lul – ly lul – lay?

Repeat Refrain after verse 3

TUNE OF 1591

2 Herod, the king,
   In his raging,
   Charged he hath this day
   His men of might,
   In his own sight,
   All young children to slay.

3 That woe is me,
   Poor child for thee!
   And ever morn and day,
   For thy parting
   Neither say nor sing
   By by, lully lullay!

   Lully, lulla, thou little tiny child,
   By, by, lully lullay.

FROM PAGEANT OF THE SHEARMEN AND TAILORS,
FIFTEENTH CENTURY

This is a modern version of one of the two carols which occur in
the fifteenth-century Coventry Pageant of the Shearmen and
Tailors. In the play, it is sung by the women of Bethlehem, just
before Herod's soldiers enter.

59

Masters in this hall

Mas-ters in this hall, Hear ye news to-day

Brought from ov-er sea, And ev-er I you pray: Now-ell! Now-ell!

Now-ell! Now-ell sing we clear! Holp-en are all folk on earth, Born

is God's Son so dear: Now-ell! Now-ell! Now-ell! Now-ell sing we

loud! God to-day hath poor folk raised And cast a-down the proud.

OLD FRENCH MELODY

2 Then to Bethlem town
   We went two and two,
   And in a sorry place
   Heard the oxen low:

   Nowell! Nowell! Nowell!
   Nowell sing we clear!
   Holpen are all folk on earth,
   Born is God's Son so dear:
   Nowell! Nowell! Nowell!
   Nowell sing we loud!
   God today hath poor folk raised
   And cast a-down the proud.

3 Therein did we see
   A sweet and goodly may
   And a fair old man,
   Upon the straw she lay:

4 And a little child
   On her arm had she,
   'Wot ye who this is?'
   Said the hinds to me:

5 This is Christ the Lord,
   Masters, be ye glad!
   Christmas is come in,
   And no folk should be sad:

The architect and carol collector, Edmund Sedding, included
'Masters in this Hall' in 'Antient Christmas Carols' which he
published in 1860. He had been given the old French carol tune
by the organist of Chartres Cathedral. William Morris was
working in the same office as Sedding, and provided the words.

owell, sing nowell

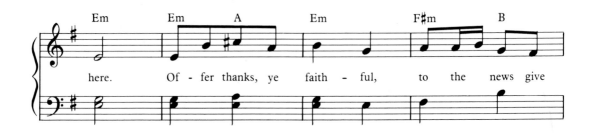

No-well, sing no-well good peo-ple ga-thered

here. Of-fer thanks, ye faith-ful, to the news give

ear. Sing we no-well, a new King born to-day.

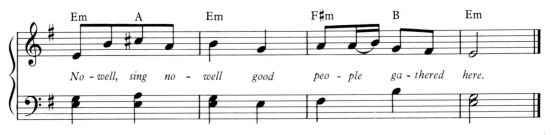

No-well, sing no-well good peo-ple ga-thered here.

TRADITIONAL FRENCH CAROL

62

2 Unto humble shepherds came the angel near;
    'Hence', said he, 'to Bethlem, be ye of good cheer.
    Seek there the Lamb of God, love's own pure ray.'
    Nowell, sing nowell good people gathered here.

3 When to Bethlehem they came in lowly fear,
    Found they gentle Mary with her son so dear.
    Heaven's mighty Lord all cradled in the hay,
    Nowell, sing nowell good people gathered here.

4 Eastern sages seek him, in the darkness drear
    By a star illumined shining forth so clear,
    Guiding them to Bethlem far away.
    Nowell, sing nowell good people gathered here.

5 Now doth our Saviour Jesus Christ appear,
    Bringing salvation promised many a year
    By his redeeming blood this happy day.
    Nowell, sing nowell good people gathered here.

TR. JOHN RUTTER

A translation of the old French carol, 'Noël nouvelet'.

Sans Day carol

Now the hol - ly bears a ber - ry as white as the

milk, And Ma - ry bore Je - sus, all wrapped up in silk: *And*

Ma - ry bore Je - sus Christ our Sa - viour for to be, And the

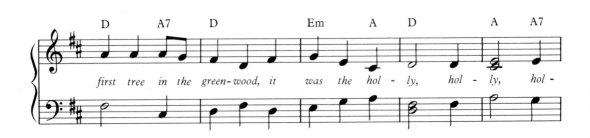

first tree in the green - wood, it was the hol - ly, hol - ly, hol -

TRADITIONAL ENGLISH CAROL

2 Now the holly bears a berry as green as the grass,
   And Mary bore Jesus, who died on the cross:

   And Mary bore Jesus Christ our Saviour for to be,
   And the first tree in the greenwood, it was the holly, holly, holly!
   And the first tree in the greenwood, it was the holly!

3 Now the holly bears a berry as black as the coal,
   And Mary bore Jesus, who died for us all:

4 Now the holly bears a berry, as blood is it red,
   Then trust we our Saviour, who rose from the dead:

'Sans', in the title, means 'Saint'. St. Day was a Breton saint
after whom a Cornish village is named, and it was from the
singing of an old man in that village that the carol, with its first
three verses, was handed on, and notated. The fourth verse is a
translation from a separate version of the carol in Cornish.

O little one sweet

O lit - tle one sweet, O lit - tle one

mild, Thy Fa - ther's pur - pose thou hast ful - filled; Thou

cam'st from heav'n to mor - tal ken, E - qual to be with

us poor men, O lit - tle one sweet, O lit - tle one mild.

OLD GERMAN MELODY

2   O little one sweet, O little one mild,
    With joy thou hast the whole world filled:
    Thou camest here from heaven's domain,
    To bring men comfort in their pain,
    O little one sweet, O little one mild.

3 O little one sweet, O little one mild,
  In thee Love's beauties are all distilled;
  Then light in us thy love's bright flame,
  That we may give thee back the same,
  O little one sweet, O little one mild.

4 O little one sweet, O little one mild,
  Help us to do as thou hast willed.
  Lo, all we have belongs to thee!
  Ah, keep us in our fealty!
  O little one sweet, O little one mild.

TR. PERCY DEARMER

*Samuel Scheidt included this German carol,
'O Jesulein süss', in his 'Tabulaturbuch' of
1650; it was later arranged by J. S. Bach.*

little town of Bethlehem

O lit - tle town of Beth - le - hem, How

still we see thee lie! A - bove thy deep and

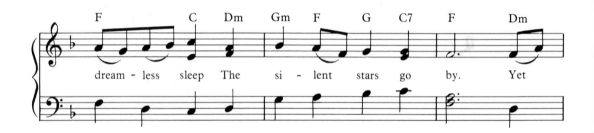

dream - less sleep The si - lent stars go by. Yet

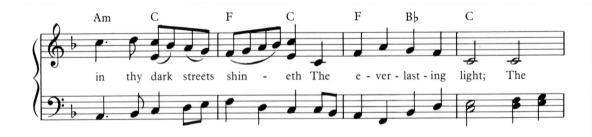

in thy dark streets shin - eth The e - ver - last - ing light; The

hopes and fears of all the years Are met in thee to - night.

ENGLISH TRADITIONAL TUNE
ADAPTED BY R. VAUGHAN WILLIAMS

2 O morning stars, together
Proclaim the holy birth,
And praises sing to God the King,
And peace to men on earth;
For Christ is born of Mary;
And, gathered all above,
While mortals sleep, the angels keep
Their watch of wondering love.

3 How silently, how silently,
The wondrous gift is given!
So God imparts to human hearts
The blessings of his heaven.
No ear may hear his coming;
But in this world of sin,
Where meek souls will receive him, still
The dear Christ enters in.

4 Where children pure and happy
Pray to the blessed child,
Where misery cries out to thee,
Son of the mother mild;
Where charity stands watching
And faith holds wide the door,
The dark night wakes, the glory breaks,
And Christmas comes once more.

5 O holy Child of Bethlehem,
Descend to us, we pray;
Cast out our sin, and enter in:
Be born in us today.
We hear the Christmas angels
The great glad tidings tell:
O come to us, abide with us,
Our Lord Emmanuel.

BISHOP PHILLIPS BROOK

This tune is derived from an English folk song. It was arranged by
R. Vaughan Williams for 'The English Hymnal'.

Once in royal David's city

Once in roy - al Da - vid's ci - ty Stood a
low — ly cat — tle shed, Where a mo — ther laid her
ba — by In a man — ger for his bed: Ma — ry
was that mo — ther mild, Je — sus Christ her lit — tle Child.

H. J. GAUNTLETT

70

2 He came down to earth from heaven
Who is God and Lord of all,
And his shelter was a stable,
And his cradle was a stall;
With the poor and mean and lowly
Lived on earth our Saviour holy.

3 And our eyes at last shall see him,
Through his own redeeming love,
For that child so dear and gentle
Is our Lord in heaven above;
And he leads his children on
To the place where he is gone.

4 Not in that poor lowly stable,
With the oxen standing by,
We shall see him; but in heaven,
Set at God's right hand on high;
Where like stars his children crowned
All in white shall wait around.

C. F. ALEXANDER

O come, all ye faithful

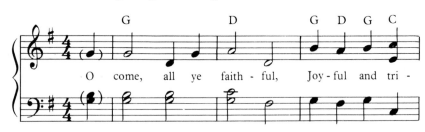

O come, all ye faith-ful, Joy-ful and tri-

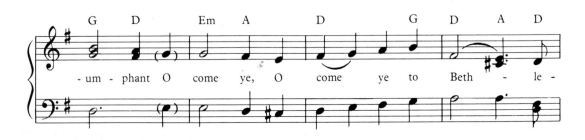

-um-phant O come ye, O come ye to Beth-le-

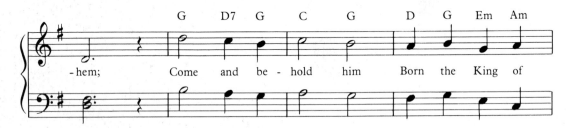

-hem; Come and be-hold him Born the King of

An-gels: O come, let us a-dore him, O come, let us a-

-dore him, O come, let us a-dore him, Christ the Lord!

J. F. WADE

72

2   God of God,
     Light of light,
     Lo! he abhors not the Virgin's womb;
     Very God,
     Begotten not created:

     O come, let us adore him,
     O come, let us adore him,
     O come, let us adore him, Christ the Lord!

3   Sing, choirs of angels,
     Sing in exultation,
     Sing, all ye citizens of heaven above;
     Glory to God
     In the highest:

4   Yea, Lord, we greet thee,
     Born this happy morning,
     Jesu, to thee be glory given;
     Word of the Father,
     Now in flesh appearing:

TR. F. OAKELEY,
W. T. BROOKE, AND OTHERS

The words are a translation of the eighteenth-century Latin hymn, 'Adeste fideles'.

The twelve days of Christmas

TRADITIONAL ENGLISH CAROL

*Although this is mostly a traditional English carol, the melody for
'five gold rings' was composed by Frederic Austin.*

ussex carol

On Christ-mas night all Christ-ians sing, To

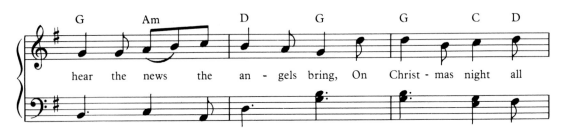

hear the news the an-gels bring, On Christ-mas night all

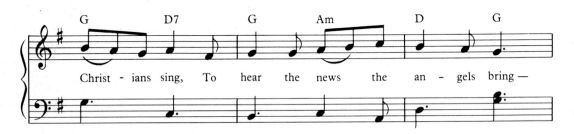

Christ-ians sing, To hear the news the an-gels bring —

News of great joy, news of great mirth,

News of our mer-ci-ful King's birth.

TRADITIONAL ENGLISH CAROL

76

2 Then why should men on earth be so sad,
   Since our Redeemer made us glad,
   Then why should men on earth be so sad,
   Since our Redeemer made us glad,
   When from our sin he set us free,
   All for to gain our liberty?

3 When sin departs before his grace,
   Then life and health come in its place;
   When sin departs before his grace,
   Then life and health come in its place:
   Angels and men with joy may sing,
   All for to see the new-born King.

4 All out of darkness we have light,
   Which made the angels sing this night,
   All out of darkness we have light,
   Which made the angels sing this night:
   'Glory to God and peace to men,
   Now and for evermore. Amen.'

 **ast three a clock**

Past three a clock, And a cold fros - ty

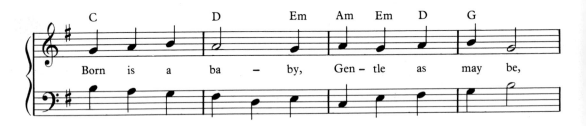

morn - ing: Past three a clock; Good mor - row, mas - ters all!

Born is a ba — by, Gen - tle as may be,

Son of th'e - ter - nal Fa - ther su - per - nal.

TRADITIONAL ENGLISH MELODY

Past three a clock,
And a cold frosty morning:
Past three a clock;
Good morrow, masters all!

2 Seraph quire singeth,
Angel bell ringeth:
Hark how they rime it,
Time it, and chime it.

3 Mid earth rejoices
Hearing such voices
Ne'ertofore so well
Carolling Nowell.

G. R. WOODWARD

The words of the refrain, as well as the melody, 'London Waits',
are traditional; the verses were written by G. R. Woodward.

Rorate coeli desuper!

Ro - ra - te coe - li de - su - per! Hea -

- vens, dis - til your bal - my showers; For now is risen the

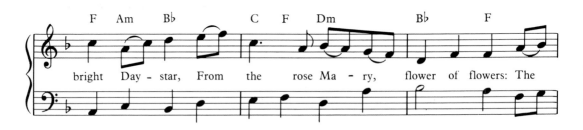

bright Day - star, From the rose Ma - ry, flower of flowers: The

clear Sun, whom no cloud de - vours, Sur -

- mount - ing Phoe - bus in the east, Is co - men of his

heav'n - ly towers, *Et* no - bis pu - er na - tus est.

TRADITIONAL SCOTTISH MELODY

2 Sinners be glad, and penance do,
  And thank your Maker heartfully;
  For he that ye might not come to,
  To you is comen full humbly,
  Your soules with his blood to buy,
  And loose you of the fiend's arrest,
  And only of his own mercy;
  Pro nobis puer natus est.

3 Celestial fowles in the air,
  Sing with your notes upon height,
  In firthes and in forests fair
  Be mirthful now at all your might;
  For passed is your dully night;
  Aurora has the cloudes pierced,
  The sun is risen with gladsome light,
  Et nobis puer natus est.

4 Sing, heaven imperial, most of height,
  Regions of air make harmony,
  All fish in flood and fowl of flight
  Be mirthful and make melody:
  All *Gloria in excelsis* cry.
  Heaven, earth, sea, man, bird, and beast;
  He that is crowned above the sky
  Pro nobis puer natus est.

WILLIAM DUNBAR

*The words are from Dunbar's 'Ode on the Nativity'. The
first line is Isaiah 45, v. 8—'Drop down, ye heavens, from
above'; the last line of each verse is 'and/for unto us a boy is born'.*

See amid the winter's snow

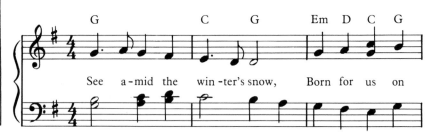

See a-mid the win-ter's snow, Born for us on

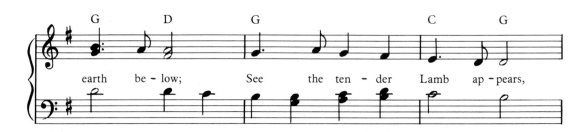

earth be-low; See the ten - der Lamb ap-pears,

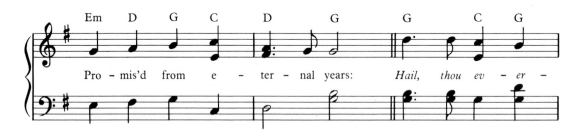

Pro - mis'd from e - ter - nal years: *Hail, thou ev - er -*

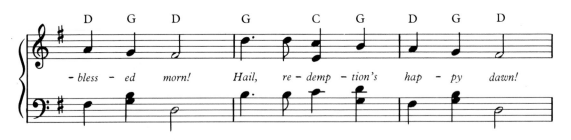

- bless - ed morn! Hail, re - demp - tion's hap - py dawn!

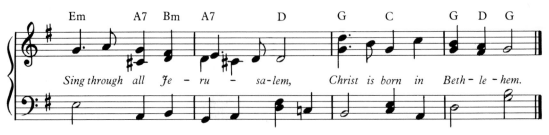

Sing through all Je - ru - sa-lem, Christ is born in Beth - le - hem.

JOHN GOSS

2 Say, ye holy shepherds, say
What your joyful news today;
Wherefore have ye left your sheep
On the lonely mountain steep?

Hail, thou ever-blessed morn;
Hail, redemption's happy dawn;
Sing through all Jerusalem,
Christ is born in Bethlehem.

3 'As we watched at dead of night,
Lo, we saw a wondrous light;
Angels singing "Peace on earth"
Told us of the Saviour's birth:'

4 Teach, O teach us, Holy Child,
By thy face so meek and mild,
Teach us to resemble thee,
In thy sweet humility:

E. CASWALL

'Christmas Carols New and Old' was an influential carol collection by Rev.
H. R. Bramley and John Stainer (both of whom were at Magdalen College,
Oxford), published in 1871. It popularized a number of traditional carols, and
also included newly-composed carol tunes, including this one by John Goss.

Shepherds left their flocks a-straying

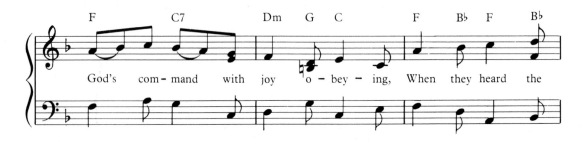

Shep – herds left their flocks a – stray – ing,

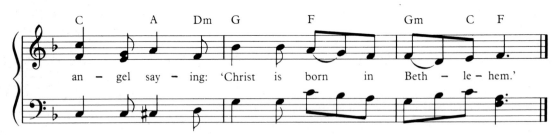

God's com – mand with joy o – bey – ing, When they heard the

an – gel say – ing: 'Christ is born in Beth – le – hem.'

OLD GERMAN CAROL

2 Wise Men came from far, and saw him:
    Knelt in homage to adore him;
    Precious gifts they laid before him:
    Gold and frankincense and myrrh.

3 Let us now in every nation
    Sing his praise with exultation.
    All the world shall find salvation
    In the birth of Mary's Son.

TR. IMOGEN HOLST

The original Latin words, 'Quem pastores laudavere', and the melody are fourteenth-century German.

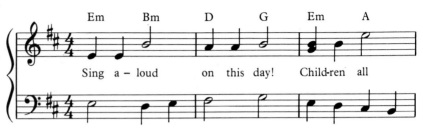

ing aloud on this day!

Sing a – loud on this day! Child-ren all

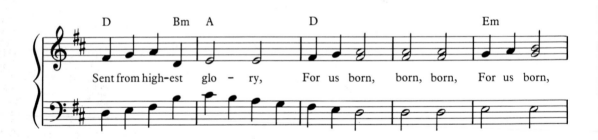

raise the lay. Cheer-ful– ly we and they Hast-en to a – dore thee,

Sent from high-est glo – ry, For us born, born, born, For us born,

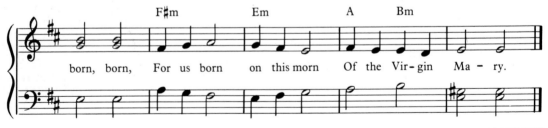

born, born, For us born on this morn Of the Vir– gin Ma – ry.

OLD GERMAN MELODY

2 Now a child he is born,
  Swathing bands him adorn,
  Manger bed he'll not scorn,
  Ox and ass are near him;
  We as Lord revere him,
  And the vain, vain, vain,
  And the vain, vain, vain,
  And the vain powers of hell
  Spoiled of prey now fear him.

3 From the far Orient
  Guiding star wise men sent;
  Him to seek their intent,
  Lord of all creation;
  Kneel in adoration.
  Gifts of gold, gold, gold,
  Gifts of gold, gold, gold,
  Gifts of gold, frankincense,
  Myrrh for their oblation.

4 All must join him to praise;
  Men and boys voices raise
  On this day of all days;
  Angel voices ringing,
  Christmas tidings bringing.
  Join we all, all, all,
  Join we all, all, all,
  Join we all, 'Gloria
  In excelsis' singing.

JOHN A. PARKINSON

*In its original Latin version,
'Personent hodie', this carol
is found in 'Piae Cantiones'
(see note on p. 31).*

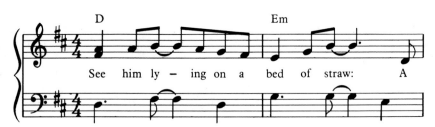

alypso carol

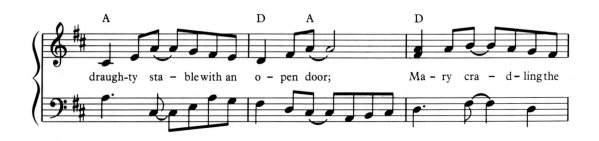

See him ly – ing on a bed of straw:

draugh-ty sta – ble with an o – pen door; Ma – ry cra – d-ling the

babe she bore— The Prince of Glo – ry is his name.

O now car – ry me to Beth – le – hem To see the Lord ap-

-pear to men — Just as poor as was the

sta — ble then, The Prince of Glo — ry when he came.

MICHAEL PERRY

2   Star of silver sweep across the skies,
    Show where Jesus in a manger lies;
    Shepherds, swiftly from your stupor rise
    To see the Saviour of the world!

    O now carry me to Bethlehem
    To see the Lord appear to men
    Just as poor as was the stable then,
    The prince of glory when he came.

3   Angels, sing again the song you sang,
    Bring God's glory to the heart of man;
    Sing that Bethlehem's little baby can
    Be salvation to the soul.

4   Mine are riches, from your poverty,
    From your innocence, eternity;
    Mine forgiveness by your death for me,
    Child of sorrow for my joy.

MICHAEL PERRY

The infant king

Sing lul - la - by! Lul - la - by ba - by, now re-

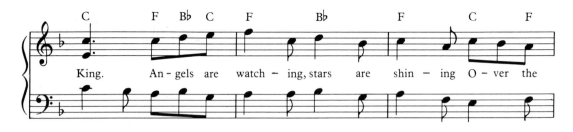

-clin - ing, Sing lul - la - by! Hush, do not wake the In - fant

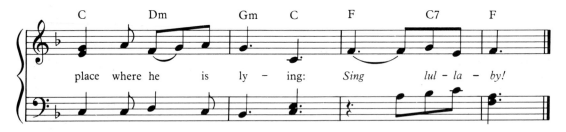

King. An - gels are watch - ing, stars are shin - ing O - ver the

place where he is ly - ing: Sing lul - la - by!

BASQUE CAROL

2 *Sing lullaby!*
Lullaby baby, now a-sleeping,
Sing lullaby!
Hush, do not wake the Infant King.
Soon will come sorrow with the morning,
Soon will come bitter grief and weeping:
Sing lullaby!

3 *Sing lullaby!*
  Lullaby baby, now a-dozing,
  Sing lullaby!
  Hush, do not wake the Infant King.
  Soon comes the cross, the nails, the piercing,
  Then in the grave at last reposing:
  Sing lullaby!

4 *Sing lullaby!*
  Lullaby! is the babe a-waking?
  Sing lullaby!
  Hush, do not stir the Infant King.
  Dreaming of Easter, gladsome morning,
  Conquering Death, its bondage breaking:
  Sing lullaby!

S. BARING-GOULD

'Oi! Betleem' or 'Oh, mi Belén' is from the Vasconia region of Spain. The original words parallel those of the English carol, 'O little town of Bethlehem'.

ilent night

Si - lent night, ho - ly night, All is calm,

all is bright; Round yon vir - gin mo - ther and child.

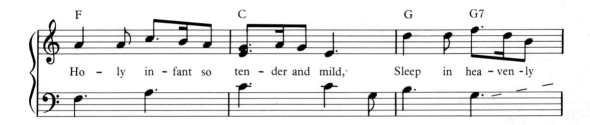

Ho - ly in - fant so ten - der and mild, Sleep in hea - ven - ly

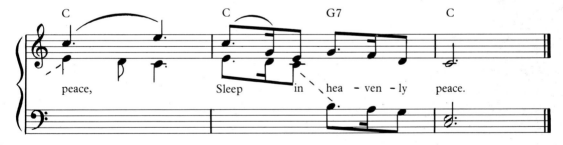

peace, Sleep in hea - ven - ly peace.

FRANZ GRUBER

2 Silent night, holy night,
Shepherds first saw the sight:
Glories stream from heaven afar
Heavenly hosts sing Alleluia:
Christ the Saviour is born,
Christ the Saviour is born!

3 Silent night, holy night,
Son of God, love's pure light;
Radiance beams from thy holy face,
With the dawn of redeeming grace,
Jesus, Lord, at thy birth,
Jesus, Lord, at thy birth.

JOSEPH MOHR TR. ANON.

abriel's message

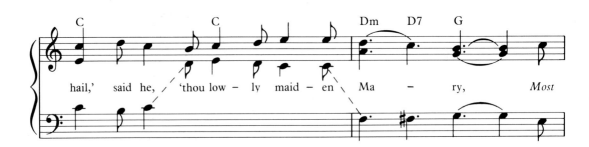

The angel Gabriel from heaven came, His wings as drift-ed snow, his eyes as flame; 'All hail,' said he, 'thou low-ly maid-en Ma-ry, Most high-ly fa-vour'd la-dy, Glo—ri-a!

BASQUE CAROL

2 'For known a blessed Mother thou shalt be,
   All generations laud and honour thee,
   Thy Son shall be Emmanuel, by seers foretold.
   Most highly favour'd lady,'
   Gloria!

94

3 Then gentle Mary meekly bowed her head,
  'To me be as it pleaseth God,' she said,
  'My soul shall laud and magnify His Holy Name.'
  Most highly favour'd lady,
  Gloria!

4 Of her, Emmanuel, the Christ, was born
  In Bethlehem, all on a Christmas morn,
  And Christian folk throughout the world will ever say—
  Most highly favour'd lady,
  Gloria!

S. BARING-GOULD

Another carol translated from the Basque—'Birjina gaztettobat
zegoen'.

 **he first Nowell**

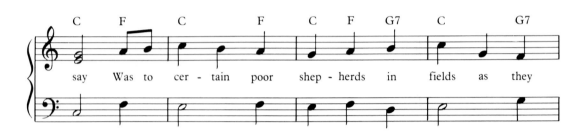

The first No - well the an - gel did

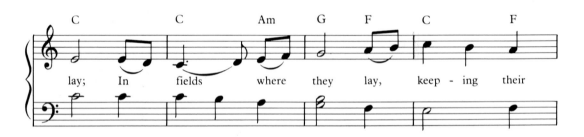

say Was to cer - tain poor shep - herds in fields as they

lay; In fields where they lay, keep - ing their

sheep, On a cold win - ter's night that was so

deep: No - well, No - well, No - well, No -

- well, Born is the King of Is - ra - el!

TRADITIONAL ENGLISH CAROL

2 They looked up and saw a star,
Shining in the east, beyond them far;
And to the earth it gave great light,
And so it continued both day and night:

Nowell, Nowell, Nowell, Nowell,
Born is the King of Israel.

3 And by the light of that same star,
Three Wise Men came from country far;
To seek for a king was their intent,
And to follow the star wherever it went:

4 This star drew nigh to the north-west;
O'er Bethlehem it took its rest,
And there it did both stop and stay
Right over the place where Jesus lay:

5 Then entered in those Wise Men three,
Full reverently upon their knee,
And offered there in his presence
Their gold and myrrh and frankincense:

6 Then let us all with one accord
Sing praises to our heavenly Lord,
That hath made heaven and earth of naught,
And with his blood mankind hath bought:

The effectiveness of this most popular of carols is hardly detracted
from by the realization that verse 2 is not strictly accurate: it was
only the Kings, not the shepherds, who saw the star.

The holly and the ivy

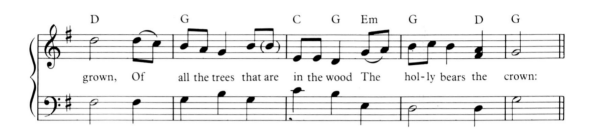

The hol-ly and the i - vy, When they are both full grown, Of all the trees that are in the wood The hol-ly bears the crown:

The ri-sing of the sun And the run-ning of the deer, The

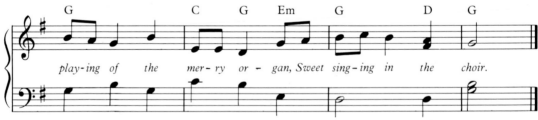

play-ing of the mer-ry or - gan, Sweet sing-ing in the choir.

TRADITIONAL ENGLISH CAROL

2 The holly bears a blossom,
As white as any flower,
And Mary bore sweet Jesus Christ
To be our sweet Saviour:

3 The holly bears a berry,
As red as any blood,
And Mary bore sweet Jesus Christ
To do poor sinners good: ·

The rising of the sun
And the running of the deer,
The playing of the merry organ,
Sweet singing in the choir.

4 The holly bears a prickle,
   As sharp as any thorn,
   And Mary bore sweet Jesus Christ
   On Christmas day in the morn:

5 The holly and the ivy,
   When they are both full grown,
   Of all the trees that are in the wood
   The holly bears the crown:

*The music and most of the words were
collected by Cecil Sharp from a singer in
Chipping Camden in Gloucestershire. There
are other versions of the words, and other
carols about holly and ivy. It is almost
certainly an example of how a non-Christian
original (in which holly symbolizes the
masculine, and ivy the feminine) became
adapted for Christian use.*

The truth from above

This   is   the truth   sent   from a - bove,   The

truth of   God,   the   God   of   love,   There – fore don't turn   me

from your door,   But   heark-en   all   both   rich   and   poor.

TRADITIONAL ENGLISH CAROL

2 The first thing which I do relate
   Is that God did man create;
   The next thing which to you I'll tell
   Woman was made with man to dwell.

3 Thus we were heirs to endless woes,
   Till God the Lord did interpose;
   And so a promise soon did run
   That he would redeem us by his Son.

4 And at that season of the year
   Our blest Redeemer did appear;
   He here did live, and here did preach,
   And many thousands he did teach.

5 Thus he in love to us behaved,
   To show us how we must be saved;
   And if you want to know the way,
   Be pleased to hear what he did say.

 owboy carol

There'll be a new world be-ginnin' from to-

-night! There'll be a new world be-ginnin' from to-night!

When I climb up to my sad-dle, Gon-na take him to my

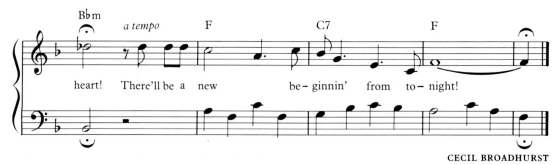

heart! There'll be a new be-ginnin' from to-night!

his endris night

This end-ris night I saw a sight, A

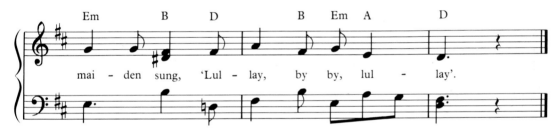

star as bright as day; And ev-er a-mong, a

mai-den sung, 'Lul-lay, by by, lul-lay'.

OLD ENGLISH CAROL

2 This lovely lady sat and sung,
And to her child did say:
'My son, my brother, father, dear,
Why liest thou thus in hay?

3 Now, sweet son, since it is come so,
That all is at thy will,
I pray thee grant to me a boon,
If it be right and skill,

4 That child or man, who will or can
Be merry on my day,
To bliss thou bring—and I shall sing,
Lullay, by by, lullay.'

*The words are found in a fifteenth-century
manuscript in the Bodleian Library in
Oxford. 'This endris night' means 'the other
night'; in verse 3, 'skill' means 'fitting'.*

The Virgin Mary had a baby boy

The Vir-gin Ma-ry had a ba-by boy, The Vir-gin Ma-ry had a ba-by boy, The Vir-gin Ma-ry had a ba-by boy, And they say that his name was Je-sus.

He came from the glo-ry, He came from the glo-rious king-dom.

He came from the glo-ry, He came from the glo-rious king-dom.

Oh yes, be–liev–er! Oh yes, be–liev–er!

He came from the glo — ry, He came from the glo- rious king-dom.

WEST INDIAN SPIRITUAL

2 The angels sang when the baby born,
The angels sang when the baby born,
The angels sang when the baby born,
And proclaimed him the Saviour Jesus.

He came from the glory,
He came from the glorious kingdom.
He came from the glory,
He came from the glorious kingdom.
Oh yes, believer!
Oh yes, believer!
He came from the glory,
He came from the glorious kingdom.

3 The wise men saw where the baby born,
The wise men saw where the baby born,
The wise men saw where the baby born,
And they say that his name was Jesus.

Unto us is born a Son

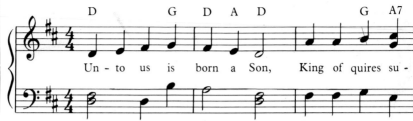

Un - to us is born a Son, King of quires su -

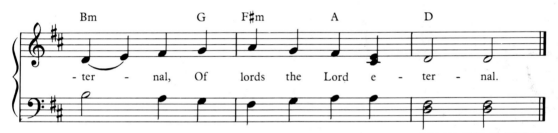

- per - nal: See on earth his life be - gun, Of lords the Lord e -

- ter - nal, Of lords the Lord e - ter - nal.

TUNE FROM *PIAE CANTIONES*

2 Christ, from heaven descending low,
Comes on earth a stranger;
Ox and ass their owner know,
Becradled in the manger,
Becradled in the manger.

3 This did Herod sore affray,
And grievously bewilder,
So he gave the word to slay,
And slew the little childer,
And slew the little childer.

4 Of his love and mercy mild
This the Christmas story;
And O that Mary's gentle Child
Might lead us up to glory,
Might lead us up to glory!

5 O and A, and A and O,
Cum cantibus in choro,
Let our merry organ go,
Benedicamus Domino,
Benedicamus Domino.

TR. G. R. WOODWARD

*In its original Latin form of 'Puer nobis nascitur', the words and original melody
are found in a fifteenth-century Trier manuscript. The tune as normally sung (and
as printed here) follows the version in 'Piae Cantiones' (see note on p. 31).*

Gloucester Wassail

Was-sail, was-sail, all o-ver the town! Our

bread it is white, and our ale it is brown, Our bowl it is made of the

white ma-ple tree; In the was - sail bowl we'll drink un-to thee.

TRADITIONAL ENGLISH CAROL

2 Here's a health to the ox and to his right eye,
Pray God send our master a good Christmas pie,
A good Christmas pie as e'er I did see;
In the wassail bowl we'll drink unto thee.

3 Here's a health to the ox and to his right horn,
Pray God sent our master a good crop of corn,
A good crop of corn as e'er I did see;
In the wassail bowl we'll drink to thee.

4 Here's a health to the ox and to his long tail,
Pray God send our master a good cask of ale,
A good cask of ale as e'er I did see;
In the wassail bowl we'll drink to thee.

5   Come, butler, come fill us a bowl of the best,
      Then I pray that your soul in heaven may rest;
      But if you do draw us a bowl of the small,
      May the Devil take butler, bowl and all.

6   Then here's to the maid in the lily white smock,
      Who tripped to the door and slipped back the lock!
      Who tripped to the door and pulled back the pin,
      For to let these jolly wassailers walk in.

*'Wassail', or 'wes hal', is old English for 'be thou whole' (or hale); it is therefore
a form of greeting, and, by extension, a festive occasion (at which ale would be
drunk from a wassail bowl or cup).*

The Coachman mixes a Christmas Bowl.

(The Huntsman is exceedingly fond of Punch.)

 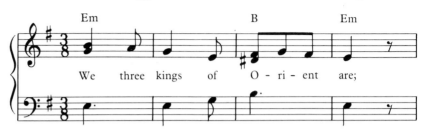

Em   B   Em

We three kings of O - ri - ent are;

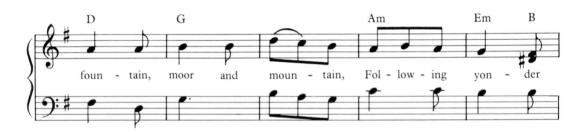

B   Em   Em

Bear - ing gifts we tra - verse a - far Field and

D   G   Am   Em   B

foun - tain, moor and moun - tain, Fol - low - ing yon - der

Em   D7   G   Em   G

star: O star of won - der, star of night,

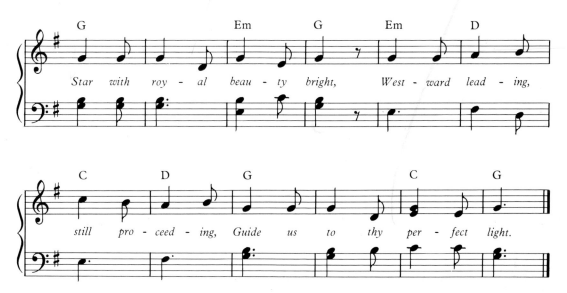

Star with roy - al beau - ty bright, West - ward lead - ing, still pro - ceed - ing, Guide us to thy per - fect light.

J. H. HOPKINS

2 Born a king on Bethlehem plain,
Gold I bring, to crown him again—
King for ever, ceasing never,
Over us all to reign:

O star of wonder, star of night,
Star with royal beauty bright,
Westward leading, still proceeding,
Guide us to thy perfect light.

3 Frankincense to offer have I;
Incense owns a Deity nigh:
Prayer and praising, all men raising,
Worship him, God most high:

4 Myrrh is mine; its bitter perfume
Breathes a life of gathering gloom;
Sorrowing, sighing, bleeding, dying,
Sealed in the stone-cold tomb:

5 Glorious now, behold him arise,
King, and God, and sacrifice!
Alleluia, alleluia;
Earth to the heavens replies:

J. H. HOPKINS

This American carol was written in about 1857
by J. H. Hopkins, who was Rector of Christ's Church,
Williamsport, in Pennsylvania.

hat child is this?

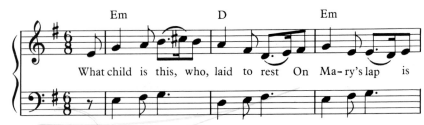

What child is this, who, laid to rest On Ma-ry's lap is sleep-ing? Whom an-gels greet with an-thems sweet, While shep-herds watch are

keep-ing? This, this is Christ the King, Whom shepherds wor-ship and

an-gels sing: Haste, haste to bring him praise, *The Babe, the son of Ma-ry.*

TRADITIONAL ENGLISH TUNE

2 Why lies he in such mean estate,
Where ox and ass are feeding?
Come have no fear, God's Son is here,
His love all loves exceeding.
Nails, spear, shall pierce him through,
The cross be borne for me, for you:
Hail, hail, the Saviour comes,
The Babe, the son of Mary.

3 So bring him incense, gold and myrrh,
All tongues and peoples own him.
The King of kings salvation brings,
Let every heart enthrone him:
Raise, raise your song on high
While Mary sings a lullaby;
Joy, joy, for Christ is born,
The Babe, the son of Mary.

W. C. DIX

 **e wish you a merry Christmas**

We wish you a mer-ry Christ-mas, We wish you a mer-ry

Christ-mas, We wish you a mer-ry Christ-mas, And a hap – py New

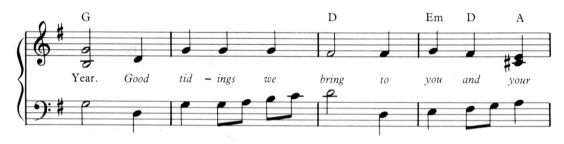

Year. Good tid – ings we bring to you and your

kin; We wish you a mer-ry Christ-mas And a hap – py New Year.

TRADITIONAL ENGLISH CAROL

2 Now bring us some figgy pudding,
Now bring us some figgy pudding,
Now bring us some figgy pudding,
And bring some out here.

3 For we all like figgy pudding,
For we all like figgy pudding,
For we all like figgy pudding,
So bring some out here.

Good tidings we bring to you and your kin;
We wish you a merry Christmas
And a happy New Year.

4   And we won't go till we've got some,
    And we won't go till we've got some,
    And we won't go till we've got some,
    So bring some out here.

In this traditional west country carol, the words should be adapted when they are sung by a single voice—'we' should become 'I', and 'us' should become 'me'.

hence is that goodly fragrance?

Whence is that good-ly fra-grance flow-ing,

Steal-ing our sen-ses all a-way? Ne-ver the

like did come a-blow-ing, Shep-herds, in flow-'ry

fields in May, Whence is that good-ly fra-grance

flow-ing, Steal-ing our sen-ses all a-way?

TRADITIONAL FRENCH CAROL

2　What is that light so brilliant, breaking
　　Here in the night across our eyes?
　　Never so bright, the day-star waking,
　　Started to climb the morning skies!
　　What is that light so brilliant, breaking
　　Here in the night across our eyes?

3　Bethlehem! there in manger lying,
　　Find your Redeemer, haste away,
　　Run ye with eager footsteps hieing!
　　Worship the Saviour born today.
　　Bethlehem! there in manger lying,
　　Find your Redeemer, haste away.

A. B. RAMSAY

*The French carol, 'Quelle est cette odeur agréable', has long been
popular outside France. The melody is used, alongside many
traditional English tunes, in the 'Beggar's Opera' of 1728.*

While shepherds watched

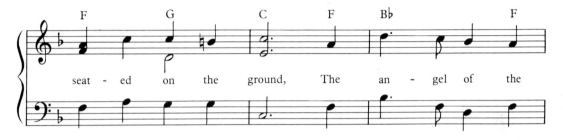

While shep-herds watched their flocks by night, All

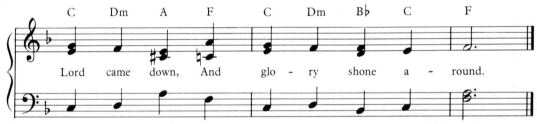

seat - ed on the ground, The an - gel of the

Lord came down, And glo - ry shone a - round.

ESTE'S PSALTER, 1592

2 'Fear not', said he (for mighty dread
Had seized their troubled mind);
'Glad tidings of great joy I bring
To you and all mankind.

3 'To you in David's town this day
Is born of David's line
A Saviour, who is Christ the Lord;
And this shall be the sign:

4 'The heavenly Babe you there shall find
To human view displayed,
All meanly wrapped in swathing bands,
And in a manger laid.'

5 Thus spake the seraph; and forthwith
Appeared a shining throng
Of angels praising God, who thus
Addressed their joyful song:

6 'All glory be to God on high,
And to the earth be peace;
Good-will henceforth from heaven to men
Begin and never cease.'

NAHUM TATE

*The words of this carol were published in 1696. They are associated with a
number of traditional carol melodies, but are most commonly sung to this hymn
tune, 'Winchester Old' from 'Este's Psalter' of 1592.*

INDEX OF FIRST LINES
AND TITLES

ACKNOWLEDGEMENTS

MUSIC

Gloria, gloria © Ivor Golby. Used by permission of A. & C. Black (Publishers) Ltd.

Down in yon forest © Stainer and Bell Ltd. Reprinted by permission.

The yodler's carol © Columbia Pictures Publications/ International Music Publications. Reprinted by permission.

How far is it to Bethlehem? Words © Miss D. E. Collins. Used by permission of A. P. Watt Ltd.

On Christmas night © Ursula Vaughan Williams. Reprinted by permission.

Calypso carol © Michael Perry. Used by permission of Jubilate Hymns Ltd.

Cowboy carol © Cecil Broadhurst. Used by permission of the Oxford Group.

Whence is that goodly fragrance flowing? Words of verses 1–3 © A. B. Ramsay. Used by permission of the Master and Fellows of Magdalene College, Cambridge.

The words of the following carols are © Oxford University Press: Deck the hall; Shepherds left their flocks; Sing aloud on this day.

ILLUSTRATIONS

The publishers wish to thank the following for permission to reproduce the illustrations which appear on the pages given below.

ii *The Adoration of the Magi*, c.1445, by Fra Angelico and Fra Filippo Lippi. Samuel H. Kress Collection, The National Gallery of Art, Washington.

1 *The Christmas Window* by John Piper. Photo © Sonia Halliday Photographs/Laura Lushington.

5 *The Nativity* by Giotto. Assisi, Italy. Photo © Sonia Halliday Photographs.

11 *The Three Kings*, sixth-century mosaic, Ravenna. Photo © Sonia Halliday Photographs.

17 *The Christmas Tree* by Albert Tayler. Alexander Gallery, London. Photo: Fine Art Photographic Library.

19 *The Virgin and Child* by Perugina. The National Gallery, London.

22 Archangel Michael, 1882, by Burne-Jones. Cattistock, Dorset. Photo © Sonia Halliday Photographs.

29 *The Nativity*, Bellieu Church at Samakov, Bulgaria. Photo © Sonia Halliday Photographs.

35 detail from the Wilton Diptych. The National Gallery, London.

39 *Father Christmas*, c.1895, by K. Roger. Victoria & Albert Museum/Bridgeman Art Library.

41 detail from the Altenberg Altarpiece. Städelschen Kunstinstitut, Frankfurt.

42 detail from mosaic of the Port of Classis, sixth-century mosaic, Ravenna. Photo © Sonia Halliday Photographs.

47 *The Snow Storm* by Goya. Prado Museum, Madrid.

49 detail of the goldfinch, Selbourne Church. Photo © Sonia Halliday Photographs/Laura Lushington.

53 detail of an angel in the tracery of the St. Catherine window by Burne-Jones. Christchurch, Oxford. Photo © Sonia Halliday Photographs.

56 *Cherub playing the Lute* by Fiorento. Photo: Scala.

63 detail of tracery by Burne-Jones, from Forden Church, Wales. Photo © Sonia Halliday Photographs.

67 *The Flight into Egypt* by Giotto. Photo © Sonia Halliday Photographs.

71 detail from *The Adoration of the Magi*, c.1445, by Fra Angelico and Fra Filippo Lippi. Samuel H. Kress Collection, National Gallery of Art, Washington.

73 *Glad Tidings* by William Spittle. Baumkotter Gallery/Fine Art Photographic Library Ltd.

77 *Snowballing* by John Morgan. Bethnal Green Museum/Bridgeman Art Library.

79 *Skaters on the lake in the Bois de Boulogne* by E. Guerard. Musée Carnavalet, Paris. Giraudon/ Bridgeman Art Library.

83 *Adoration of the Magi in the Snow*, 1567, by Breugel. Oskar Reinhardt Collection, Switzerland.

85 *The Seven Joys of Mary* by Hans Memling. Alta Pinakothek, Munich.

87 *The Angel* by Burne-Jones. Glasgow Art Gallery and Museum.

91 *Angel with his Lute* by Melozzo da Forlì. Photo: Scala.

92 a praying angel by William Morris. Cattistock, Dorset. Photo © Sonia Halliday Photographs/ Laura Lushington.

95 *The Archangel Gabriel*, seventh-century mosaic, Kiti, Cyprus. Photo © Sonia Halliday Photographs.

99 *Birds in the Snow with Holly and Mistletoe* by E. J. Detmold. Photo: Fine Art Photographic Library Ltd.